MY JOB OFFER NEGOTIATION SKILLS ARE STRONG

I think

I0463272

...SO WHY DIDN'T I GET ANYTHING I ASKED FOR?

Easy guide for students and recent grads to evaluate and negotiate the details of a *job offer!*

STACIE GARLIEB

ISBN: 1449966411

ISBN-13: 9781449966416

The anecdotes and comments in this book are based on the author's
experiences, enhanced by commentary from colleagues. It is not the
intent of the author to represent such content as true or to offend or
cause malice to any individual or organization. Any resemblance in this
book to an actual person, living or dead, is purely coincidental.

TABLE OF CONTENTS

I think

INTRODUCTION

You successfully answered the questions in a phone interview, a live interview (or several) and the company just called to make you a job offer! Getting an offer is exciting – so how do you know if it's a 'good' offer? What are the important parts of an offer to understand? How can you negotiate parts of an offer?

When and how do you notify other companies when you accept an offer?

The 'we' in the book is referring to a combined collaboration of recruiters, HR managers, and hiring managers who are currently in positions hiring students and recent grads. 'We' make offers to students and recent grads every week, and have heard almost every question about an offer asked in good and bad ways.

Understanding what a company is truly offering you (beyond a paycheck) is important for you to evaluate which job opportunity is going to fit your needs at the time. Go through each section of the book step by step and figure out what areas you will use at this point in your career. After you start your post-graduation path, you can refer back to this book for tips as you receive and negotiate promotions, lateral positions between departments, or relocation.

My understanding of what to do when
I 'get the call' is clear **I think** …

In **'My interview skills are good I think …_so why didn't I get the job offer?'_** © one key to successfully working through the phone interview process is to make sure are in the 'right place' at the 'right time' for the interview. And just like that situation, taking a call from an employer about a job offer when you are walking between classes, driving down the freeway, or sitting in a loud restaurant is not a good strategy.

The best way to make sure you are ready when you 'get the call' is to not answer your phone if you don't recognize the number. Recruiters and hiring managers will leave you a message. We know you have class and a life and it's not a big deal if we talk to you right then or in an hour when you are in a better place to have a professional conversation.

Before you call the person back, make sure you have these things in front of you:

- Pad of paper to take some quick notes
  - Look at the list in the next section of the book for some basic categories of information you may be told via phone about an offer

- Job description that you applied and interviewed for
  - This lets you verify the title of the job and some basic information

+ Any specific notes you took at Information Sessions or during the interviews about the compensation package

The first thing the hiring person will tell you is 'We would like to make you an offer'. They may pause to see your reaction – don't get too crazy, but this is a good time to say 'Thank you, I am very excited to hear from you'. Next, the person will give you some very topline information about the position – usually title, base salary, whether you receive a 'benefits' package, and what else you have to do to officially secure the job.

It is very normal for companies to ask for the following as 'contingent on completion for employment':

+ Background check
+ Drug test
+ Driver's License check (depends on the job)
+ Completion of an I-9 Form
  – verification of ability to work in the US

Once the person finishes telling you the basics of the offer, it's your turn to respond. Unless you have already decided **not** to accept the offer, you can respond with a simple statement like "I appreciate the offer. Could you please send me the details in email or fax so I can see what questions I have?". This allows you to see the offer in writing and then figure out what you want to do – ask questions, negotiate parts, accept, or reject it.

At this point, the hiring person will probably give you a deadline of when they need to hear back from you. Management does this so we can hire our next choice if you reject the offer. It's also a way to get you to commit faster and then we can move forward to the other responsibilities we have in our jobs. Don't panic over the deadline, just wait until you get the offer in writing and then move forward with what your next step should be.

• • •

My knowledge of what to look for in an offer is good I think ...

Every job offer has some basic parts, but each offer will also have different 'extras' or 'benefits' based on the level of responsibility for the position, size of the company, and current market trends for the industry or job title. Here are the most common parts of an entry or secondary level job offer:

- Salary – hourly, base (annual or weekly or bi-weekly), stipend – paid at the end of a given time period
- Medical benefits
  - Medical could include general medical, dental, vision care or a combination of any of those

- Vacation/Sick day benefits
- Insurance benefits – short and/or long term care
- 'Bonus' compensation
  - Usually based on achieving goals and could be tied to several different criteria

- 401K and/or retirement/pension plan
- Mileage reimbursement or Car Allowance or Company car
- Business Expense reimbursement
- 'Signing bonus'
- Relocation allowance or reimbursement
- Start Date
- Geographic location of the position

- Timing for performance evaluation and review of merit increase to base salary (quarterly, annual)

Not every job offer will have all of these parts. It's important to do some homework in advance to know what is reasonable for your position. For example, a salesperson would probably have some form of 'bonus' to increase motivation to sell more, while someone in an operations position in a manufacturing plant may not. Remember that some of these things may be offered in the second or third level of a company's career path also. Several Fortune 500 companies that used to give entry-level salespeople a car in the past are now giving mileage reimbursement or a car allowance until the person reaches a management level.

Let's look at a few of these items in more detail so you can see some general guidelines and differences:

- **Salary**
  It doesn't really matter whether it's hourly or weekly or bi-weekly, as long as the total amount at the end of a month meets what you are looking for.

- **Medical benefits** (usually only post-graduation opportunities or almost full-time jobs in school)
  Two very important things to look for here:

  1) When do the benefits start?
     If you are a student, you may be on Student Health Insurance or your parent's plan. Be sure you don't have a 'gap' between when you aren't eligible for whatever plan you are on and the start of the company plan.

     It's not unusual for a company to start benefits after 90 days of employment ('the probationary period'), so plan on what you can do to bridge your coverage during this time.

2) What exactly is covered?
Dental benefits may not be included, vision may not be included, etc. so again be sure if you need a certain level of coverage that you are looking for that in the offer.

◆ **Vacation/Sick Day benefits**
Some companies will give vacation time after a certain amount of 'time in the job'. This could also be considered 'accrued vacation'. So, if you start the position in June, possible you 'accrue' one day of vacation after each month of employment – which means that on December 1st you would have six days of 'accrued vacation'.

Other companies will give a flat number of vacation days each year, based on number of years you have worked there. Two weeks is pretty typical for a company to offer at entry-level. Be aware though, the company can set a time period and different times during the year that vacation is or is not approved.

Companies also can set the number of allowable sick days per year. If this is part of the offer, then it's important to understand what happens if you come down with the Swine Flu and can't work for a week. If you only get four sick days per year, does the fifth day get taken out of your vacation time? Don't get too hung up on the details of this, but it's good to understand just in case.

- **401K/pension and Mileage reimbursement or car allowance or company car**
  Each organization will have set policies on these based on the structure of the company. We will address this more in the "negotiable" and "non-negotiable" section of the book.

- **'Signing bonus'** (post-graduation positions)
  Not every offer will have one of these, but they are becoming more common across industries and especially in larger companies. The signing bonus is intended to motivate you to commit to the company earlier in the school year. It allows the company to plan more accurately for how many openings are going to need to be filled each semester for entry level positions.

  Most signing bonuses come with a 'catch' – the document you "sign" will usually state that if you leave the company within a certain period of time (most often 12 months), you have to pay the 'signing bonus' back to the company. This isn't a big deal as long as you are evaluating the offer completely and making a decision to accept the offer based on the total package. Most of you won't be moving between companies in the first year post-graduation!

- **Relocation allowance or reimbursement**
  Similar to the 'signing bonus' there can be a document which says repayment is due if you leave the company before a certain period of time. In the 'negotiable' section of the book we will discuss more details around what would be appropriate to ask about on relocation packages.

- **Timing of performance evaluation and merit increases**
  These are also specific to the company's policies. More details on these benefits will be in the 'non-negotiable' and 'negotiable' sections of the book.

Overall, the more information you can get about the details of an offer, the better prepared you will be to evaluate what is 'good' and what could potentially be clarified or negotiated.

• • •

My ability to evaluate what is 'negotiable' is strong I think ...

Not everything is 'negotiable' in a job offer. Some parts of the offer are going to be 'fixed' based on company policy. Remember that companies have to offer 'fair' compensation packages and benefits to employees, so some things may be formal policy for everyone.

Here are some general guidelines on how to determine what may be 'negotiable':

- Information on salary and bonus structure was shared at a group session or posted in the job description
  - If a company has openly shared a flat (as opposed to a range) salary or bonus publicly, the potential to negotiate this is going to be less. By putting it in writing the company has set the expectation to you in advance to avoid going through negotiation.

- Someone in the interview process reviewed details of the health benefits package with you already
  - Medical and dental and vision benefits themselves are usually not negotiable since companies establish those through large health insurance companies. Timing of the start of benefits may be negotiable though!

- You asked a specific question about performance-based evaluations in the interview process

- In the 'Questions to Ask in an Interview', you asked the hiring person about when you would be evaluated on performance and they said you would get an annual review and merit increases are based on that. If you already know that, then it is probably company policy so the organization can plan set timing and percentages for salary increases (outside of promotions). Asking for the company to go outside of policy to review your performance earlier is not realistic.

The purpose of asking for the offer in writing is to see the specifics of the compensation package – and compensation includes EVERYTHING you receive from a company, not just money. When you are looking at the written offer, it's important to figure out what information is there and what may be 'missing' that you need to ask questions about.

Maybe there is 'Health Benefits' but no details about timing for the start of coverage. Vacation time and how you get it may not be listed. Participation in the 401K or pension plan might be vague. Consider all of the items on the list above and see what gaps there are in the written offer.

Negotiation doesn't have to be 'asking for more'. It could be clarifying and requesting a different timeline. You may 'negotiate' a later start date so you can take some time and travel post-graduation. Possibly you have a trip scheduled later in the year and you want to have extra days of vacation 'accrue' to be able to use them then. Maybe the signing bonus is less than you know is being offered by other companies in the industry that year – do your homework on this one first – then you could possibly request additional compensation here.

Here are some commonly 'negotiated' parts of an offer – be careful though, not everything is up for discussion and you want to choose the ones that are most important to you to ask for first!

- **Salary**
  - This is only safe to do if you know from the company that there is a 'range' offered and your skills would justify being given a higher salary in the range than what was offered to you.

- **Timing of health benefits to start**
  - Company policy or contracts with the healthcare company may or may not allow for this.

- **Vacation allowance timing**
  - May or may not be negotiable depending on the company policy. The best time to negotiate this is if you already have a trip planned and you can establish that right away with the company to have the time off. Negotiating to get vacation early without a plan could seem unnecessary.

- **Mileage vs. car allowance vs. company car**
  - Each company will have policies around this that will change from year to year. It never hurts to ask if you could get a car allowance instead of a company car. Especially if your parents are buying you a new car for graduation!

- **Signing bonus amount**
  - Be aware that this will most likely have a 'repayment' factor for leaving the company before a certain time of employment

- **Relocation allowance or reimbursement**
  - This also will most likely have a 'repayment' factor for leaving the company early.
  - Relocation amounts may be 'fixed' by geography or distance relocating ('non-negotiable' section)
  - Since relocation is usually handled by an outside company, the amounts may also be restricted based on the contracts with the provider.

I think

- **Start date**
    - Delaying your start date (if you are a June grad and you want to start in August) might be ok, but remember that the company projects several dynamics around when they offer you a start date, including salary costs, training class timing, allocation of workload in departments, etc.
    - You can ask for a delay but a pre-planned reason will give you a greater chance to get it.

- **Timing of performance review**
    - The size of the organization will depend on how negotiable this point is – small to medium size companies may be able to determine timing on a sliding 'start date' scale.

It's also important to note that you don't need to negotiate anything in some cases! Companies may not give you all the information you need and then it is definitely important to ask questions to understand the offer completely. If the offer has all of the parts you need to make a career decision, then don't 'make up' something to negotiate. Be realistic as to what the company has offered you and what is important to your evaluation in joining an organization.

• • •

My determination of what is
'non-negotiable' makes sense **I think** ...

'Non-negotiable' items in an offer are also dependent on the size of the organization, company dynamics that year, industry standards, and other factors like geography. Salary may be 'non-negotiable' because the company has set levels for the position in given geographies each year. Maybe the company just contracted with X car manufacturer and Y car insurance company to get company cars for all of the entry-level people – chances of getting a car allowance would be pretty low in this case.

Here are some general 'non-negotiable' parts of an entry or secondary level position:

- **Level of Health Benefits**
  - Most companies negotiate contracts with insurers on these, so they are set for all employees.

- **Sick Day Benefits**
  - If the company has listed allowable number of sick days, then it is a company policy which is non-modifiable. It's good to understand these policies in advance of acceptance of the offer.

- **Insurance Benefits**
  - These are contracted most of the time through a third party and will be standard for all employees in a company.

- **'Bonus' compensation**
  - Unless you are entering a commission based position (and even those are usually non-negotiable percentage based), don't try to negotiate this. Companies do fiscal projections on scales and bell curves for bonus payouts so they are fixed in advance.

- **401K and pension/retirement plans**
  - Timing to contribute into these, amount you can contribute, and whether a company even offers these is already pre-determined through contracts with providers and federal guidelines.

- **Mileage reimbursement**
  - The amount of mileage reimbursement is set by the federal government each year. Most companies will follow this guideline.

- **Car allowance**
  - If you are offered a car allowance you probably won't be able to negotiate the amount at the entry level, but at higher levels there may be an opportunity to do this.

- **Company car**
  - Organizations that offer a company car contract with large manufacturers to get discounts. Sorry, but the odds of getting a Lexus when the company contracts for a Malibu are not good.

- **Business expense reimbursement**
  - You will either get this, or not. It really depends on what your job description is and what company policy is on what is considered a 'business expense' or not. Meals when travelling, accommodations, office supplies, etc. could be included. Instead of negotiating on this, it's a good idea to

ask questions about what is generally classified as 'business expense'.

+ **Geographic location of the position**
    - This may be negotiable as long as they haven't asked you previously where you prefer to be located. Companies plan this out before they extend offers, so you may not have a choice.

• • •

My evaluation of who I should talk to about negotiable points is on target I think...

Who called and offered you the job? In larger organizations, a human resources person will make the actual offer because those people are experts in answering questions about the different parts of the compensation package. Some companies have the hiring manager (who you will be reporting to) call – they can tell you how excited they are to have you 'join the team'. Smaller companies may have the Owner contact you to give the offer and then have an office manager or other department head follow up with the details.

Ultimately, the person who calls you is the first one to follow up with once you have read the written offer. Before you do that, here's what you need to prepare:

- Notes on a pad of paper with the categories of the offer that you have questions about
  - This includes items that you need more information on, not necessarily items to negotiate

- List – in order of importance to you – of parts you want to negotiate
  - You have to plan out what you are going to ask for. Don't just ask for 'a later start date' – have an exact date you want to change to AND a rationale for why you are asking for it.

- This doesn't mean you have to give graphic details on where you are going to travel to for a delayed start date. Just be general in explaining that the trip is already planned.

When you call the person who made you the offer, establish that you are calling to get more information on parts of the offer. At that point, they may tell you to call someone else, which is fine. If not, then start the conversation letting them know you have taken time to review the offer and show appreciation for receiving it. Go through the items you have questions about first and take notes! If you are going to try and negotiate, then start with the most important item first.

Remember, the company can always tell you NO to the things you ask for. The better you have planned a rationale for the request, the higher your chances you will have of getting it, or at least moved closer to what you want. It's very important to ASK for negotiated parts of the offer – don't be perceived as 'telling or demanding' something. The difference is using "could I" or "is it possible to" instead of "I need to" or "I can't" when you make the request.

The person may have to 'get back to you' on items you want to have modified. That is perfectly normal. Some items might be 'non-negotiable' and you won't know until you ask. Once you get answers back on your questions and (if applicable) negotiated points, then it's decision time.

At this point, if you are interviewing with multiple companies – which most of you will be – then you have to start evaluating a number of variables. Keeping accurate notes throughout the interview process with each company will help to make the decision time much easier and less complicated!

· · ·

My timeline for making a decision is appropriate for the company I think...

You've talked to the right person and asked questions about the details of the offer. After presenting your reasons for wanting to negotiate on a couple of items, you were given reasons you could or could not have what you asked for. Now the company wants to know if you are 'in' or 'out'.

When the person first made you an offer, they probably told you when the company 'needed to hear back from you'. The time between receiving the written offer and asking questions or negotiating (or both) may have gone past the original timing they wanted an answer in. If that's the case, you have a shortened period of time to make a decision.

The key to knowing what your timeline for acceptance or rejection of an offer depends on your communication with the person you are having offer discussions with. Too many students go MIA during the offer evaluation process and leave employers guessing on when they will know when the person is going to commit or not. That's why we have set deadlines for acceptance – it limits our delay to contacting our alternate candidate with an offer.

As long as you are realistic in getting back to the company (within a week is about the maximum), you will be ok. If the organization sets a deadline though, don't push it or you will look unprofessional. Waiting until noon on a Friday, when Friday is the final day to accept or reject an offer, just is not necessary unless you were waiting to hear from your 'first choice' company to get back to you and that was as soon as you heard from them. By giving an answer as soon as you can to a company, you are being respectful of their hiring process and allowing them to move forward one way or another.

• • •

My views on what is realistic for an entry-level position are accurate **I think**....

As a student who is going to graduate or a recent graduate, it's important to be realistic on what companies will be offering you at the entry-level. Everyone would love to make six figures, have a big car allowance, make crazy money in bonus or commission, get a raise every six months, and have full benefits with a 401K, pension, and company stock. For your first or second post-graduation opportunity, this is not realistic. Here are the basics that are very realistic for most post-graduation opportunities:

- ◆ Salary that is fair for the market value of the responsibilities of the job, including industry standards and consideration of cost of living in the geography of the area
  - Yes, someone living in CA or NY would probably earn more than someone living in ID with the same job description and title in the same company. Each company gets to set what those differences are annually.
  - A great place to get a general range for this information is CBSalary – it's a search program through Career Builder® which takes into consideration geography, responsibilities etc. Just be aware that entry-level positions may have a little lesser range. Most of the data in that system will come from positions that may be beyond entry-level.

- ◆ Benefits or an option to pay for benefits through the company
- ◆ Vacation time

- Reimbursement for company expenses (office supplies if 'at home' office, mileage, business travel etc.)
- Performance review after a set period of time

Those are fairly standard categories for an entry-level position. Each industry will have other offer parts that would be considered 'fair and equitable'. Look at similar opportunities with other companies that are posted through Career Services or job search engines or company internal websites to identify what else may be realistic for your specific field.

• • •

My process for rejecting an offer

is professional I think ....

After you have taken the time to evaluate the offer details, you have decided that the company, the position responsibilities or the key parts of the offer are not what you want. Here are the most important things to remember about rejecting an offer:

- Respect the company's timeline and let them know as soon as possible
  - Remember that they may have a 'second choice' candidate that the management would go to in case you did not accept. The earlier you reject the offer, the higher the odds that the company can still fill the position with a qualified candidate that has also been through the interview process completely, rather than having to start all over.

- Always reject an offer via phone – do not leave a voice mail – talk to the person live. Email is also not appropriate.
- Let the company know why you are rejecting the offer
  - If the reason is that you have another offer that you have decided to accept, you don't have to go into the details, but let them know that. Wouldn't it be great if companies would tell you why they chose someone besides you to interview? Give a broad reason like "I have decided to accept another offer that will allow me to relocate back to the Midwest".

- If you are rejecting because they didn't meet your negotiation points, then you can simply say "I have chosen to pursue other opportunities at this point that will offer a different compensation package."

- Don't burn any bridges!
  - Depending on the field you are going into, you may end up working with, or for, the management whose offer you reject, someday. Thank the recruiter or hiring manager for the opportunity to learn more about the organization and for their time during the interview process. That goes a long way toward keeping your professionalism in the industry for the future.

When you have contacted the person to reject the offer, it is appropriate to follow up in writing via a brief email. Again, this should show appreciation for their time. Another tip includes emailing any managers that you interviewed with and letting them know your decision and appreciation for their time. Those managers may have openings in the future that they could consider you for depending on how you manage the rejection of the offer. If you email the managers, wait until a day after you speak with the recruiter or HR person – this lets them do 'their job' and inform management of your decision.

• • •

My acceptance of an offer shows
my business skills I think ....

It's a good offer, and you are ready to commit – call the person you discussed the offer with. Make sure your questions have been answered first so you feel confident about the position and the compensation package. When you make the call, remember to:

- Thank the person for the opportunity to work for the company.
- Ask when and how the company wants you to complete the final steps in the offer process
  - This potentially includes a drug test, physical, authorization for a driver's record check, signing bonus or relocation package agreement form, and/or completion of an I-9 form.

- Confirm your start date and location/time you are to be 'at the office' (worksite etc.).

What if the company wants you to 'sign' an agreement of acceptance? Whether you are receiving a signing bonus or not, it is very common for companies to ask for a written confirmation which acknowledges that you have accepted the offer. This verifies that you have read the offer an understand all of the sections.

Don't confuse this with a 'contract'. Until you have shown up for your first day of work (your first official day 'on the payroll'), you are not employed. If you accept a signing bonus or relocation package funds prior to your first day, and you for whatever reason do not go to work at that company, you could be responsible for paying back that money.

Just as you would for rejecting an offer, follow up with an email to the person you spoke with to confirm your excitement about the opportunity and details about next steps and start date.

• • •

My notification to other employers that I am 'off the market' is appropriate **I think** ....

Notifying other companies that you have started the interview process with that you are not going to be available to continue in the process is a really important step. This goes along with 'not burning bridges' in the rejection section of the book. The reality is that every industry's recruiters and hiring managers could somehow know each other. We potentially are members of similar organizations, interact at national conferences, or network with each other to set standards for hiring practices and compensation.

That means if you 'blow off' a company, there is a high probability that other companies in the field could hear about it. It doesn't take long to notify people when you aren't going forward with their company, so here are some different situations and specific tips to have the most professional approach:

- You have been contacted by the company for a phone interview, but have accepted another offer before the phone interview takes place
  - In this case, you could email the person who scheduled the phone interview with you and simply state: "I have decided to accept an offer from another organization at this time. Thank you for considering my qualifications for the position."

- You have had a phone interview and are 'waiting' to hear back about the company scheduling a live interview with you

- Same scenario as above, but in this case, you should call the person you had the phone interview with if you have their number. If you don't have their phone number, then you could email them.

♦ You have had a live interview and are 'waiting' to see if you are going to the second round of interviews
  - In this situation, it is VERY important to contact the person who held the live interview with you via phone. Don't leave a message on voicemail!
  - If you absolutely cannot reach the person who interviewed you, you could contact the human resources person (if applicable) and talk live to them.

♦ You have been through all of the interviews, but have not received an offer yet
  - Probably this company would be a 'second choice' for you if you had an offer from them. It's important to contact the company asap once you accept another offer so you keep the 'door open' for possible positions in the future. Again, live contact to the person you have had the most contact with through the interview process at this point.
  - Also, you could contact the managers you interviewed with a day later to thank them for their time in the interview process.

♦ You have been through all of the interviews, and have an offer from another company
  - This is the most difficult situation because you are probably pretty interested in this company at this point. You may even have had a hard time choosing between companies. Contact should be live with at least the person you have been communicating with the most during the process.

- Depending on how much of a connection you made with the other people who interviewed you, you could contact them via phone or email to show appreciation for their time and keep the door open for the future.

· · ·

'My job offer negotiation skills are strong I think... so why didn't I get anything I asked for?' ©

Here's a final checklist to help make sure you are managing the offer evaluation, rejection, and acceptance processes with the highest level of professionalism:

- Before returning a call to an employer who may be making an offer, you are in the 'right place' and have a pad and pen to take notes
- During the 'offer call', ask for written details of the offer to evaluate all of the parts
- After receiving the written offer, evaluate each of the parts and see what questions need to be answered about details or more information in different sections
- Determine what is 'negotiable' vs. 'non-negotiable'
- Contact the person who made the offer within a reasonable amount of time
- Follow up to reject or accept ASAP
- Inform other companies once you have accepted an offer that you are no longer available

After you accept an offer, celebrate! Congratulations on successfully working through the interview process. Remember that interviewing is a lifelong skill and negotiation will be a skill that you will use throughout your career – for promotions, moves into different departments in a company, changes in industries, or even geographic moves within an organization.

• • •

Extra Resources:

Career Services/Career Center Departments

- Depending on the college or university, you may have access to classes on negotiation skills.

www.bestresumebuilder.com

- If you want to use a program which will walk you through, step by step, in less than a half hour, check out this resource. Created specifically for collegiates and recent grads, it's specific and easy to use. This may help you focus your interview answers to the 'bullet points' on your resume.

• • •

INDEX

I think

• • •

Other Books in the Ithink Career Skills Series:

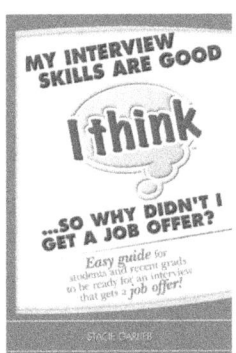

Coming Soon in the Ithink Career Skills Series:

'My social networking skills are amazing Ithink....so why can't I find a job?' ©

AND

'My interview preparation was detailed Ithink...so why didn't I feel prepared once I got there?' ©

Available Online and In Stores Fall 2010!

• • •

ACKNOWLEDGEMENTS

Thank you to the collegiates and post-grads who have tried different methods and successfully gained negotiated parts of their offers over the past 20 years.

Thank you to Mark and Tyler for your support during the writing process.

. . .

ABOUT THE AUTHOR

Stacie Garlieb is the author of 'My resume is perfect I think ... so why didn't I get the interview?'© and 'My interview skills are good I think...so why didn't I get a job offer?' © As the President of Successful Impressions, LLC., she assists collegiates and recent graduates with career search processes and skills. She has been featured several times on NBC television and KFYI radio during morning and evening news with interview tips. In partnership with University of Phoenix, Stacie is the creator and presenter for the 'Career Workshop  Series' on resume building, interview preparation, interview skills, social media networking, and 're-careering' and transition in the workforce.

Stacie has been a seminar speaker for 'Build Your Career Event' (Career Builder/University of Phoenix) and the Arizona Women's Expo. Her career search tips and interview skills advice have been published in national sorority and university alumni publications. Through group presentations and one-on-one coaching on all career search related topics, she has worked with public and private college students nationally since 1991. In collaboration with businesses in various fields, she actively develops internship programs and recruits at public and private universities as well as career fairs.

Stacie was invited by California State Sacramento and University of the Pacific to act as a Career Consultant to the career services departments. She developed the Career Fair Training Program for University of the Pacific, and assisted in writing the "Career Services Interview Skills" guide. Over more than twenty years, she has worked for Fortune 500 organizations in sales, marketing, and management positions with recruiting responsibility after earning her Bachelor of Science from Arizona State University.

If you would like to know more about Stacie Garlieb's company or her seminars please visit her website at www.successfulimpressions.net

• • •

www.ingramcontent.com/pod-product-compliance
Lightning Source LLC
Chambersburg PA
CBHW051257170526
45165CB00004B/1753